MORAL DILEMMAS

A RIGHT TO LIFE – AND DEATH?

KENNETH BOYD

Evans

EVANS BROTHERS LIMITED

First published in 1999 by
Evans Brothers Limited

Evans Brothers Limited
2a Portman Mansions
Chiltern Street
London W1M 1LE

© Evans Brothers Limited 1999

ISBN 0 237 51877 5

Editor: Su Swallow
Design: Neil Sayer and Tinstar Design
Production: Jenny Mulvanny
Picture research: Victoria Brooker

British Library Cataloguing in Publication Data

A right to life and death?. - (Moral dilemmas)
    1. Right to life - Juvenile literature
    2. Right to die - Juvenile literature
    3. Medical ethics - Juvenile literature
    179.7

ACKNOWLEDGEMENTS

For permission to reproduce copyright material, the author
and publishers gratefully acknowledge the following:

Cover (central image) Robert Harding Picture
Library (background image) Larry Mulvehill/
Science Photo Library **page 7** Edward Parker/
Hutchison **page 8** Rex Features **page 11** Sarah
Errington/Hutchison **page 12** Simon Fraser/
Science Photo Library **page 14** Rex Features
page 16 Simon Fraser/Princess Mary Hospital,
Newcastle/Science Photo Library **page 18**
Keith/Custom Medical Stock Photo/Science
Photo Library **page 19** Rex Features **page 20**
Orde Eliason/Link **page 21** Rex Features **page
23** Rex Features **page 24** Sarah Errington/
Hutchison **page 27** Hank Morgan/Science Photo
Library **page 28** BSIP/Laurent/Aube/Science
Photo Library **page 29** D Phillips/Science Photo
Library **page 31** Robert Harding Picture Library
page 32 Rex Features **page 34** Rex Features **page
36** Damien Lovegrove/Science Photo Library
page 38 Mark Clarke/Science Photo Library
page 40 Hank Morgan/Science Photo Library
page 43 Hank Morgan/Science Photo Library
page 44 James King-Holmes/Science Photo
Library **page 45** Larry Mulvehill/Science Photo
Library **page 47** Mehau Kulyk/Science Photo
Library **page 48** Florence Durand/Rex Features
page 50 Rex Features **page 52** Alison Wright/
Robert Harding Picture Library **page 53** John
Greim/Science Photo Library **page 55** Rex
Features **page 58** Robert Harding Picture Library

CONTENTS

1. RIGHTS, LIFE AND COSTS

Kate is pregnant, but she doesn't want to have a baby. Jane can't become pregnant, but she and Mark want to start a family. Alice has to have dialysis twice a week but would do better with a kidney transplant. Michael needs a heart operation, but may not get it. Mr Smith has had two strokes and doesn't want to be kept alive the next time his life is in danger. Miss Brown is losing her memory and tells her doctor she wants to be helped to die.

Has Kate a right to an abortion? Or has the foetus a right to life? Have Jane and Mark a right to medical help in starting a family? Have Alice and Michael a right to the treatment they need or want? Have Mr Smith and Miss Brown a right to die?

What are rights?

Rights are what we think we ought to be able to expect – from other people, or from life itself. When we say we have a right to something, we mean that someone else should help us to get it, or at least should not prevent us from getting it. Some rights are things everyone agrees about and are protected by the law.

Should a woman have a right to an abortion?

Everyone has a right to be considered innocent unless proved guilty, for example, and also a right to basic social security, education and health care. But having a right to basic health care does not mean having a right to every possible medical treatment, and a right to health care is not the same thing as a right to health. We have a right to expect other people not to harm our health by polluting the atmosphere or injuring us, and we ourselves can avoid an unhealthy lifestyle. But neither we nor other people can guarantee that we will always stay fit and healthy. Sometimes there is nothing more that doctors and nurses can do to restore a patient's health, and if they keep on trying they may be depriving other patients of the help to which they have a right.

> *Should the right to life of the unborn child be of paramount importance rather than the rights of the two living adults involved?*

A right to life?

Has everyone a right to life? In the past, especially during war or famine, some people had fewer rights than others. Slaves, prisoners, foreigners, even babies and old or poor people were sometimes regarded as less than human. But when societies became richer, and people began to think carefully about their own religious and moral beliefs, more and more became convinced that everyone has a right to life. Fifty years ago, when the Nazis murdered hundreds of thousands of mentally ill and physically disabled people, as well as millions of Jewish people, the rest of the world refused to accept the Nazis' excuse – that such people were 'unworthy of life'. Nowadays, when society says that everyone has a right to life, it is insisting as strongly as possible that there are no excuses for murder and genocide or 'ethnic cleansing' and that those responsible must be pursued and punished by

A poisonous smog envelops Mexico City, one of the most polluted cities on Earth. How do we decide between our right to breathe clean air and our desire to enhance our lives with things which pollute: cars, fridges, and so on?

national and international law.
To say that everyone has a right to life means that no one's life should be ended against their wishes, or because it suits someone else. But what about someone who does wish to die, as Miss Brown says she does? Or what about the foetus growing inside Kate, which may not yet have any wishes at all? Is helping someone who wants to die – euthanasia or 'mercy-killing' – the same thing as murdering them? Does a foetus or an embryo have as much right to life as any other human being? Are all the abortions that take place daily in hospitals 'genocide of the unborn'? Some people say 'yes' to these questions, others say 'no'. The strong views on both sides show that these are vital questions. We need to decide for ourselves what we think about them.

Is it right to think of other human beings as less worthy of a right to life? These refugees in Rwanda were the intended victims of genocide at the hands of their fellow countrymen, in direct contravention of the most basic declaration of the United Nations.

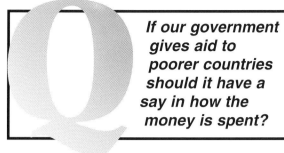

If our government gives aid to poorer countries should it have a say in how the money is spent?

The cost of living?

Doctors nowadays can save the lives of many more people than in the past. A commonly used drug or a routine operation may be all that is needed to prevent someone from dying and get them back to normal life. But sometimes people's lives are saved and they never get back to normal. They survive death, but only at the cost of ongoing physical or mental suffering, or in some cases at the cost of being unconscious or unable to talk with other people. Some people who suffer in this way feel that life is still worth living despite everything. Other people, in the same circumstances, feel that they have had enough. The Nazis would have said that none of their lives were worth living. But the Nazis were interested in themselves, not in the people they were talking about. Whether someone's life is still worth living, despite all the costs, is a question that can be answered only by that person.

Universal Declaration of Human Rights, United Nations, 1948

'. . . recognition of the inherent dignity and of the equal and inalienable rights of all members of the human family is the foundation of freedom, justice and peace in the world. . .' [from Preamble]

'All human beings are born free and equal in dignity and rights. They are endowed with reason and conscience and should act towards one another in a spirit of brotherhood.' [Article 1]

'1. Everyone has the right to a standard of living adequate for the health and well-being of himself and his family, including food, clothing, housing and medical care and necessary social services, and the right to security in the event of unemployment, sickness, disability, widowhood, old age or other lack of livelihood in circumstances beyond his control.

2. Motherhood and childhood are entitled to special care and assistance. All children, whether born in or out of wedlock, shall enjoy the same social protection.' [Article 25]

Basic Documents on Human Rights
3rd edition, Oxford, Clarendon Press 1992

But what if the person concerned cannot answer the question, because they are confused or unconscious, for example? Should their life be prolonged by costly care and treatment, or should they be allowed to die? There is no simple answer. It depends on what is wrong with the patient and what chances there are of improvement or recovery as a result of treatment. In some cases doctors can be reasonably sure that the chances are too good to miss, in others that they are too poor to try. But even the most experienced doctors can't always be sure. Taking life and death decisions for someone else is never easy.

Q *Doctors and nurses sometimes know, from long experience, that the chances of saving a patient's life are very small. What should the doctors do if the patient's family ask them to do everything possible to prolong the patient's life?*

Scarce resources

These decisions are particularly difficult when there are not enough resources to go round. In some poorer countries, even simple forms of medical treatment and ways of preventing disease, such as immunisation which could save countless lives, are still not available to large numbers of the population. There are many reasons for this – war, famine, corruption and governments spending money on arms rather than health. But international aid can help the situation, and many people now believe that the best way to mark the millennium would be for richer countries to cancel the crippling interest payments which many of the poorest countries have to pay on the loans they received in the past.

Even in the richest countries there are sometimes not enough resources to save the lives and improve the health of everyone who could benefit. New and better forms of medical and surgical treatment are being developed all the time. Years ago, for example, when someone was told that they had cancer, it was regarded as a death sentence. Nowadays many forms of cancer can be treated successfully. Many people with cancer (or with HIV infection, which until very recently usually led on to AIDS) have years of life to look forward to. But the treatment they need is often expensive, and the more effective such treatments become, the more people there are who can be helped by them.

Sometimes, when a new treatment is particularly expensive, a health authority with only a limited amount of money to spend may decide that it can't afford to provide it. This means that some people with a right to health care may not get it. As a result some of them may die and others will continue to suffer from conditions which could be treated

Q

Should richer countries ensure that basic, low-cost preventative health care is provided to all in poorer parts of the world?

A public health scheme in Zaire. Poor countries have limited resources available and also find it difficult to provide services which will reach into the more remote areas of their often very large countries.

more effectively. That may be avoided if the people concerned can afford private medicine, or if a public campaign raises sufficient funds, or if the government gives the health authority a larger budget. But often none of these alternatives are available; and if publicity in the media forces the health authority to provide the treatment, it may then not have enough money left over to provide treatment needed by other patients, who also have a right to it. When everyone has a right to life and to health care but there is not enough to go round, whose rights or needs should come first?

A young boy in northern India receiving a vaccine against measles. Schemes like these are very effective ways of preventing disease and death in childhood.

Infant Mortality and Life Expectancy

Of every 1,000 babies born in Britain, the number who die before reaching their first birthday fell from 150 in 1900, to seventy in the 1930s, to eight in the 1990s. In Africa, where families are much larger, far fewer babies survive and many more mothers die in childbirth. Those children who do survive can expect to live for fifty to fifty-five years, compared to seventy to eighty years in a country like Britain. In developing countries, poverty, malnutrition, pollution, accidents and violence are major causes of disease and death. Many fatal diseases could be prevented or cured by vaccination or simple medical treatment.

Oxford Medical Companion, Oxford, OUP 1994

Rights and wrongs

Nowadays there is often no agreed right or wrong way of answering questions about who gets priority. In modern democracies everyone has a right to take part in the decision-making which will affect their own lives. Patients have a right to be consulted by doctors about their individual treatment, and the public

has a right to be consulted by health authorities and governments about health care priorities. But different people have different views. When we disagree about the rights of the mother versus the rights of the foetus, for example, or about whose needs should come first when there is not enough to go round, are there any ways of helping us to resolve these disagreements?

Two things can help. One is to make sure we have got the facts right. Don't simply accept what other people – especially people with strong views – say. Try to listen to both sides of the question, and then weigh up for yourself the facts and arguments on both sides.

The other thing that can help, when we are thinking about rights and wrongs in health care, is to keep in mind four widely agreed basic ethical principles. They are: first, to avoid harm; second, to do good; third, to respect everyone's views; and fourth, to be fair to everyone. If we can find a way of resolving our disagreements which does all four of these things, that will be the ideal answer. Often the ideal answer just isn't possible. But if we try to do as many of these things as we can, as well as we can, it is more likely that we will get nearer to it.

2. ABORTION

Kate is forty years old and has just discovered she is pregnant. She already has three children, two girls and a boy, aged seventeen, fifteen and thirteen, respectively. A few years ago she and her husband John, a chef, opened a small restaurant. It does well, but only because they both work very long hours. A month or so ago, rushing to catch the plane for their first weekend abroad for several years, Kate forgot to pack her oral contraceptives. She thought she was unlikely to conceive because of the time of the month, but when they got back home she was suspicious. She carried out a pregnancy test, and it was positive.

Kate and John discuss what they should do. All of their income goes on family expenses and the children's education. They can't afford to pay someone else to take on Kate's work while she has the baby, and if they are going to have another child, Kate wants to bring it up herself, as she did with the others before she went back to work.

It is rare today to find families in the developed world as large as the one here. This is partly due to women having more access to methods of birth control.

They could give up their business and John could try to find another job. But he would earn a lot less and they feel this would not be fair to their other children at this stage in their education. So, reluctantly, they decide to go to their doctor to ask if Kate can have an abortion. The doctor thinks that Kate and John have taken a responsible decision, and sends Kate to a hospital specialist who agrees to terminate her pregnancy. After further discussion with the doctors, Kate also has a sterilisation to prevent her having any further children.

> *In Britain about one in three women will have an abortion at some time in her life, usually before the age of 25: about 170,000 abortions are carried out every year and the abortion rate is 13 per 1000 women aged 15–45. In the US the rate is 24 per 1000 and in Russia, 124 per 1000.*
>
> Professor James Drife, Consultant Obstetrician and Gynaecologist, in Oxford Medical Companion, *Oxford, OUP 1994*

Early abortion

Because Kate went to her doctor early in pregnancy, there were no serious legal or medical objections. In Britain, abortion is allowed up to

> *Should a foetus be treated like a baby when it begins to look like a baby, or when its mother begins to think of it as a baby?*

the twenty-fourth week of pregnancy if the doctors believe that the risk of 'injury to the physical or mental health of the pregnant woman or any existing children of her family' is greater if pregnancy goes on than if it is terminated. From a medical point of view, the risk to a woman's health is very much less if she has an abortion during the first twelve weeks than if she continues with the pregnancy until a baby is born.

No one in Britain has a legal right to 'abortion on demand'. But many doctors feel they have no moral right to refuse requests from women or couples who have thought carefully about it, provided they ask early enough. In Kate's case, because she is older, there is also a greater risk that pregnancy could endanger her health or that the foetus could be abnormal.

If Kate became an invalid or had a disabled baby this could have a harmful effect on her mental health or the mental health of her other children.

Later abortion

After twelve weeks, although an abortion may still be legal, doctors are less willing to agree to it. The operation is more dangerous, and more unpleasant. After twenty-four weeks, abortion is illegal unless there is a risk to the life, or of 'grave permanent injury' to the health of the pregnant woman, or there is a 'substantial' risk of a 'severely handicapped' child being born. The reason for this change at twenty-four weeks is that soon after that time, with medical help, a foetus might be able to survive outside the womb. It might be born prematurely (twelve or more weeks before the normal time). Doctors and nurses will then be expected to do everything they can to save the baby's life, unless he or she is so unlikely to survive or so severely disabled that this will only cause suffering.

This tiny baby is about twenty-three weeks old and is thirteen weeks premature. The baby is breathing with the aid of a respirator.

> *. . . abortion is a necessary evil, one that must be tolerated and supported until such time as better sex education, more effective contraception, and a more just social order make possible fewer troubled pregnancies. And even then, there will still be some justifiable reasons for abortion; it will never disappear.*
>
> Dr Daniel Callahan, Ethicist, in Abortion: Understanding Differences, *New York,* Plenum Press 1984

The law and abortion

The law in most other European and North American countries nowadays is similar to that in Britain. Abortion is allowed up to twelve weeks, and later if the risks are very serious. But in some countries – Spain, Portugal and Ireland, north and south of the border, for example – it is not allowed at any time unless the risks are exceptionally serious, or in some cases if the pregnancy is the result of rape. Until the 1960s, abortion was against the law almost everywhere. But in Britain alone there were tens of thousands of illegal abortions, carried out by unqualified people in unhygienic conditions. They were often dangerous and many women actually died as a result. Legalising abortion in hospital has made it safer. But it also means that more women now have abortions. Some doctors and many other people believe that abortion is now too easy, and that it should either be forbidden or at least made more difficult.

Should a man have a right to prevent a woman aborting his child?

In practice, it has been shown that women usually take great thought and pains to identify and minimise the harms, balancing different or competing harms in a nuanced way when considering whether to keep or terminate a new pregnancy. Such down-to-earth examples of compromise might put ethicists, politicians, campaigners, and religious leaders to shame, and convert the general question to the particular: "How much should this possible new life matter, in this situation and at this stage?"

Professor Roger Higgs, General Practitioner, in New Dictionary of Medical Ethics, London, BMJ 1997

Something or someone?

The main objection to abortion is the belief that an embryo (up to twelve weeks) or foetus (after twelve weeks) is a human being with a right to life, just like a new-born baby. There is no very obvious difference between a new-born baby and a normal foetus. By twenty-eight weeks its heart is beating, it can open its eyes and move around in the womb. But well before that – soon after sixteen weeks, when it is the length of an adult's hand – the foetus can hear, and its mother may begin to feel it moving inside her. Earlier still, around twelve weeks, its arms and legs may begin to move. At that stage the foetus is only half the length of an adult's thumb, but it has already begun to look like a human baby. In fact, from the moment when the father's sperm fertilises the mother's egg, creating an embryo, to the moment when a baby is born, its growth is a continuous process. Scientifically speaking, there is no one point in this process when you can say for sure that the embryo or foetus has changed from being something into being someone.

Bundles of cells or potential people?

There is no clear scientific dividing line in the development from embryo to foetus to baby. But that applies only to those which survive. The great majority of embryos, about three in every four that have been fertilised, die during the first week, mostly before they can be implanted in the womb. Many people think it just isn't common sense or natural to say that these short-lived bundles of cells are human beings with a right to life; that they are persons. Those which will survive, of course, are potential persons. But a potential person may not have the same rights as an actual person. Small children, for example, are potential voters but they do not have the right to vote. This doesn't mean that an embryo, especially after it has begun to grow in the womb, is no more than a growth in a woman's body which can just be cut out if she doesn't want it. But while an embryo is more than a growth, many people believe that it is less than a person.

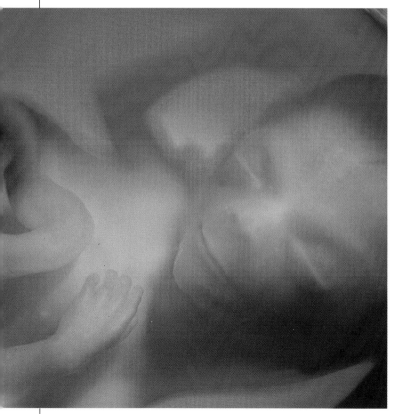

A foetus at twelve weeks. The facial features are clearly human and the fingers of the left hand can be seen.

A moral question

When do you become a person? There is no scientific answer to this because it isn't a scientific question. It is a moral question – a question different people may answer in different ways. Some people say you are not a person until you begin to think of yourself as an individual. Most non-human animals for example are not persons. But if this view is right, babies during the first year or so of their lives may not be persons either. That too doesn't seem common sense or natural. Other people think that a foetus becomes a person when its mother starts thinking of it as a person. But different mothers do that at different times. In the past, many people thought the crucial moment was 'quickening', the time around sixteen weeks when the mother may begin to feel the foetus moving.

In many countries abortion is a highly emotive issue; in the United States it has even led to violence. Is it moral to harm other, living humans in order to protect those not yet born?

Religious views

Another way of thinking about when the foetus becomes a person is the religious one – that it becomes a person when God thinks of it as a person. The writer of the Psalms in the Bible says that God knew him in his mother's womb. But many later Jewish teachers thought that the foetus did not become a person until it was born. Five or six hundred years ago the Catholic church taught that a foetus does not become truly human (does not have a human soul) until sometime between forty and ninety days (or five to twelve weeks). Before that time it has an existence at first more like that of a plant and then of a non-human animal – as if something like the whole history of evolution took place over again in the development of each individual. That view probably seemed sensible and natural to many people at the time. But the Roman Catholic Church eventually gave it up because some of the scientific ideas it used to support it were disproved. Its official view nowadays is that the embryo is a human being with a right to life from conception. Many Buddhists, Muslims, Hindus and Evangelical Christians also believe this. But many other religious people aren't so sure.

St Peter's in Rome, the heart of the Vatican. The Roman Catholic Church is opposed to birth control, believing that the embryo is a human being with a right to life.

Rights or the best thing?

When there is disagreement about an important moral or political question, each side often feels very strongly that their own view is the only right one. Abortion is sometimes presented as a debate between 'the woman's right to choose' and the 'unborn child's right to life'. But things are rarely so simple when real people are involved. Kate, for example, believes in God, but she also believes that it wouldn't be fair either to her family or to herself to go ahead with having another baby, and she thinks of the embryo at this stage as something like the miscarriage or natural abortion that happened a couple of years after her last child was born. If

Pro-choice demonstrators in the United States. Abortion has always existed, but before proper, legal methods were permitted many thousands of woman died at the hands of unqualified amateurs. Is it better never to know life or to experience it as an unwanted and unloved person?

she had been younger, or if she and John had been better off, or if she hadn't discovered she was pregnant until very much later, she might have decided not to have an abortion. She is sorry that it has to happen. It would have been better if she had remembered her pills. But she believes that having an abortion is the best thing she can do in the circumstances for everyone concerned, and because she is religious she believes that if she really has done the wrong thing, God is merciful. For Kate, the main thing now is to go on doing her best for the people she loves.

> **Foetuses can be tested to see whether they will develop inherited bowel cancer, the lung disease cystic fibrosis or muscular dystrophy, which causes muscle wasting. Within five years they could be screened for conditions ranging from most other hereditary cancers to Alzheimer's disease, behavioural disorders and even dyslexia. The question for doctors and parents is: in deciding which babies to terminate, where should the line be drawn?**
>
> Sunday Times, *June 1996*

More difficult choices

Other people think differently and sometimes have to face more difficult choices. Kate was lucky to have the support of John and to know that her work was important for her family. But other women have to decide what to do on their own, often at a very much younger age than Kate. An unmarried student may become pregnant after having sex with a boy at a party where she has too much to drink, and may be so afraid of telling anyone that she leaves going to her doctor until after twelve weeks. She could decide to have the baby and then have it adopted. Many people gave their baby for adoption in the past and many childless couples want to adopt. But who will look after the student during her pregnancy? Will she be able to give her baby up when it is born? Will she be able to get back to her studies afterwards? The answer to these questions depends on all sorts of things the student herself doesn't yet know, and also on how far other people are able and willing to help her – her parents for example, or perhaps the father of the child. The father has no legal right to prevent her having an abortion, and if she decides to keep the child he may or may not be the best person to help her bring it up.

Abortion and disabilities

Older women may also have problems Kate did not have to face. A couple with two children may be looking forward to the birth of their third. But tests done between the tenth and fifteenth week of pregnancy may show that the baby is likely to have Down's syndrome. Children with Down's syndrome have mental disabilities, but how severe these are varies, and some families cope with this more successfully than others. Some couples, who know how much-loved and loving a child with Down's syndrome can be, may decide to go ahead with the pregnancy. Others may feel that they and their existing children are just not able to do this and may ask for an abortion.

> *If abortion were legally more difficult, would there be more babies for childless couples to adopt?*

Children with Down's syndrome can lead happy and fulfilling lives. But sometimes parents fear that the child will be difficult to cope with. What should doctors say if asked to perform an abortion?

> *If women understood that late abortions don't have to create lasting trauma, fewer would feel obliged to give birth to a handicapped child.*
>
> *Mother of unborn Down's syndrome son*

Depending on their own feelings, beliefs and experiences, the doctors they ask may also have different views on what is the right thing to do in these circumstances.

Tests done at various stages before birth may also show a variety of other disabilities of varying seriousness in the foetus. In some cases the 'substantial' risk of a 'severely handicapped' child being born will be so great that everyone involved agrees that, even at a late stage, an abortion is the best thing. But what if the test for a very disabling disease shows that the foetus may grow into a baby who will not develop the disease until he or she is over forty? Or what if the test shows that the foetus is female and the parents desperately want a boy, perhaps because they already have several female children and in their culture having a male heir is terribly important, or the cost of providing for another girl's marriage is just too great? The risk to the mother's mental health, some people might say, could be very serious here too.

Q *How do you think people with a disability feel when foetuses with the same disability are aborted?*

In countries where there are insufficient resources to go round, should women use methods of birth control in order to limit the numbers of children exposed to disease, malnutrition, poverty, war and famine?

> *At what stage should the fertilised egg be considered a human being with rights which might override those of its mother?*

> *Only ten years ago, most doctors believed the newborn baby could not feel pain. Now we know a "child" still too young to be born can feel pain.*
>
> Glenys Roberts, Daily Mail, *July 1996*

No ideal solution

There are no simple answers to these questions. Abortion is always a difficult decision for the woman and family involved. But there have always been abortions and there probably always will be. In some societies unwanted babies were killed after birth, and even today this sometimes happens in very poor countries. In an ideal world, every baby would be a wanted baby and everyone who did not want a baby either would not have sex or would use effective contraception. But we don't live in an ideal world. All we can do is try to make it better. Contraception for some people, and not having sex for others, is always better than abortion. But people who have an abortion may be doing the best thing in their circumstances.

Most doctors and parents understand this. In Britain, doctors who don't agree with abortion usually say so and ask the woman or couple to see another doctor who will help. Doctors are also allowed by law to give confidential advice about contraception to people under sixteen who really can't talk to their parents about it. The doctor will probably try to persuade them to discuss it with their parents, but won't force them to if there are really good reasons for not telling their parents and if the young person understands the advice the doctor is giving.

> *If unborn children can feel pain, should abortion be illegal?*

> *Doctors do not wish to inflict suffering on foetuses, but to relieve the suffering of women.*
>
> Ann Furedi, Birth Control Trust

3. FERTILITY TREATMENT

Jane and Mark married three years ago. Two years ago they decided to start a family and stopped using contraceptives. But Jane still hasn't become pregnant. When they go to see their doctor, she tells them there could be several different reasons for this. The simplest is that it might just take longer. About a quarter of couples who want to have a baby don't succeed in the first year, but by the end of the second year most of them do. Or it might be something more complicated. Some couples – less than 10 per cent – who would like to have children, either never have them or can do so only with medical help.

In vitro fertilisation

The problem may be something to do with the man's sperm, or with the woman's eggs, which prevents the sperm fertilising an egg and producing an embryo. When that happens, some couples can be helped by fertility drugs, or by medical techniques which help the sperm get to the egg and fertilise it. Or a blockage in the woman's

With money needed for so many urgent cases, should nature just be allowed to take its course if couples are unable to produce children?

In the last five years there has been a major advance in the treatment of male infertility. . . Using sophisticated instruments and specially designed optics on microscopes, it has been possible to select an individual spermatozoon and inject it directly into the egg. This treatment, called Intra-cytoplasmic Sperm Injection, or ICSI, has been remarkably successful. Even men producing very few sperm – perhaps less than 1 per cent of normal numbers – are now treatable. . . some 4,000 babies have been born using this approach.

Professor Robert Winston,
Genetic Manipulation, *London, Phoenix 1997*

This greatly magnified image shows the delicate act of inserting a single sperm directly into the egg using a tiny needle (right) while the egg is held steady by a pipette (left).

fallopian tubes may prevent the egg from being fertilised and getting to the womb where it can grow. The blockage may be difficult to remove. But another way round this problem is *in vitro* fertilisation or IVF. Eggs taken from the woman are fertilised in a laboratory glass dish (*in vitro*) by sperm taken from the man, and the embryo is then replaced in the woman's womb. When IVF was first used successfully, in 1978, many people asked if it was right to produce 'test-tube babies'. But as more and more healthy babies were born following IVF, it became widely accepted.

Depending on the problem, there are different ways doctors can help

a couple like Jane and Mark to have the baby they are hoping for. But sometimes no medical treatment works. The man's sperm or the woman's eggs may just not be capable of producing an embryo. Or for various medical reasons the woman may not be able to carry it successfully to birth. Even if that happens, there are still ways of helping the couple to have a baby. But these ways are more controversial.

> *IVF has a relatively low success rate and in the best clinics only 20 per cent of treatment cycles result in pregnancy. Moreover, the need to transfer more than one embryo simultaneously to improve the success rate means that many IVF treatments have the unpredictable result of a multiple pregnancy – twins, triplets or even quadruplets. This means that the risks of losing the entire pregnancy are greatly increased – humans were not designed biologically to produce a litter.*
>
> Professor Robert Winston,
> Genetic Manipulation, *London, Phoenix 1997*

Microtubules or straws of frozen donor sperm held in a liquid nitrogen storage tank. Is it right for one person to father several offspring in this way?

Donor insemination

Suppose Mark cannot produce sperm with the capacity to fertilise Jane's eggs. In that case they might decide to use donor insemination, also known as AID (artificial insemination by donor). Sperm is provided by another man (a donor), and the doctor places this in the woman where it can fertilise her eggs. A great number of babies have been born this century as a result of AID. Neither they nor their parents normally know who the donor is, and in Britain they are registered as the child of their mother and her husband. In the past, many never even knew they had been conceived by AID. Nowadays, when they reach eighteen or are intending to marry, they can find this out from the authorities, although not who the donor was. But nowadays, too, many parents feel it is best to tell them earlier.

Many people conceived by AID feel like many children who are adopted – the loving parents who brought them up in a good home just *are* their parents. But some children feel differently and want to know, or dream about, who the donor was. And sometimes, if the couple are unhappy together, the fact that another man was involved can create extra problems. So if AID is the only way for a couple like Mark and Jane to have a baby, they need to think ahead.

Should someone who has been born as a result of AID be allowed to find out who the donor was?

A sperm about to penetrate the surface of the egg. When it gets through and fuses with the nucleus a membrane will form on the egg as a barrier against other sperm.

> *Anonymous gamete donation is only one aspect of the new reproductive technology that fails to accord the respect that is due to the child. Well-intentioned though donors may be, they are essentially abandoning responsibility, both emotional and financial, for their children.*
>
> Jacqueline Laing, The Independent, *July 1998*

Egg and embryo donation

But what if it is the other way round, and there is no problem with Mark's sperm, but Jane cannot produce eggs? In this case another woman might donate eggs. These would be fertilised, using IVF, by Mark's sperm. The embryo would then be placed in Jane's womb where it can grow into a baby who would be registered as the child of Mark and Jane. In some ways this is like AID. But both parents are more involved in the biological processes, so there may be fewer potential difficulties for the child or for the parents.

A third possibility is that Jane cannot produce eggs and Mark cannot produce sperm. This doesn't happen very often. But when it does, eggs from a female donor can be fertilised, using IVF, by sperm from a male donor, and the embryo placed in the womb of the mother who will give birth to the baby. That baby, some people might say, has four parents. The donors are his genetic parents (the man and woman his genes come from), Jane is his birth and social mother (the woman who carried him in her womb, gave birth to him and is bringing him up), and Mark is his social father (the man who is officially registered as his father and also is bringing him up). This could cause family problems later, like those with AID. But once again a lot depends on how the children and parents get on with one another. If a couple like Jane and Mark want children so much that they are prepared to go through all these complicated procedures, there is a good

> *... given the commercial and scientific interests at stake, it is quite possible for the modern clinician to prey on the unjustified fears of some women that their lives are meaningless or unfulfilled unless they have children. The point ... is that one can lead a good and fulfilling life without children.*
>
> Jacqueline Laing, The Independent, *July 1998*

chance that they will also create a loving home and that their children will feel that they are their real parents.

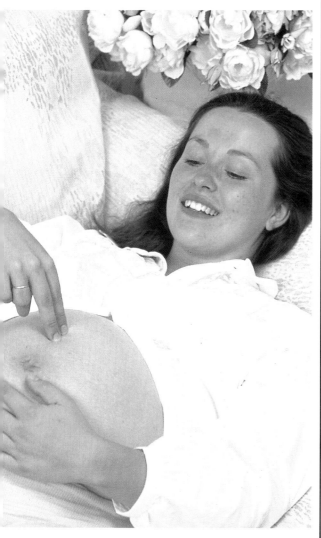

A mother-to-be feeling her baby's movements in the womb. Is it right for a child to be conceived with complex origins, potentially confused as to its identity when it has no straightforward 'father' and 'mother'?

Surrogacy

Children born as a result of IVF or sperm or egg donation have a very special relationship with their mother because she carried them in her womb and gave birth to them. But sometimes a woman can't do this. There may be some problem with her womb, or it may not be safe for her to be pregnant because she has a medical problem such as a heart condition. If Jane has either of these problems, another way that she and Mark can be helped to have a child is surrogacy.

The word 'surrogate' means a substitute or a deputy. A surrogate mother is a woman who carries an embryo, and the foetus it grows into, through pregnancy. Then after birth she hands the baby over to a couple who will bring it up. In the Book of Genesis in the Bible, Sarai, the wife of Abram, cannot have a child. So that she can have one, she tells her husband to have a child by her maid, Hagar. Abram does so and it leads to all sort of problems caused by jealousy between Hagar and Sarai. Surrogacy is rather like a modern equivalent to this. But the embryo is conceived as a result of AID or IVF, not as a result of sex between the people involved, as in the case of Abram and Hagar.

Different forms of surrogacy

Surrogacy can take different forms. The simplest (called 'partial' surrogacy) is a bit like what happens when the man can produce sperm but the woman cannot produce eggs and the eggs are donated by another woman. But in 'partial' surrogacy, the female donor also carries the child. If Jane not only can't carry a child, but also can't produce eggs, Mark's sperm can be used, as in AID, to fertilise the eggs of a surrogate mother who also carries and gives birth to the child. More complicated forms (called 'full' surrogacy) involve placing embryos created by IVF in the surrogate mother's womb. Depending on the problem, the embryos can be created from sperm and eggs provided by the mother and the father, or by the father and an

Should people who lead socially unacceptable lifestyles be denied fertility treatment?

A woman with a child conceived for her by a surrogate mother. If this form of child-bearing is permitted, is it much different to children being bought and sold like any other commodity?

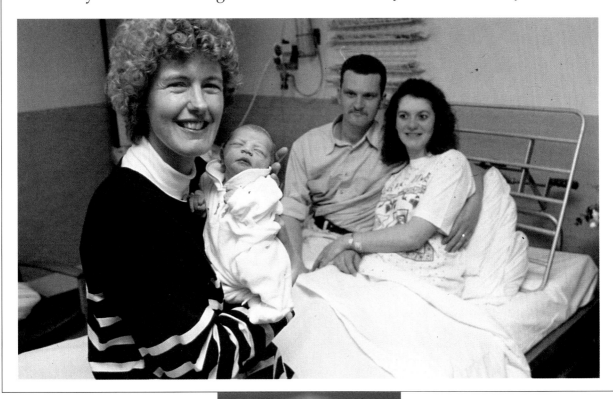

egg donor, or by the mother and a sperm donor, or by a sperm donor and an egg donor.

> **Who are the real parents – the genetic parents, the birth parents or the social parents?**

Legal and financial arrangements

If Jane and Mark need the help of a surrogate to have a child, they will have to think very carefully about what is involved, and so will the surrogate mother. Surrogacy is not against the law in Britain if it is arranged privately and not commercially. But couples usually pay 'expenses' – maybe around £10,000 – to a surrogate mother, and they may have to pay a private clinic if AID or IVF is needed. In Britain and many other countries, fertility treatment is not very freely provided by national health services because life-saving or pain-relieving treatments take priority. Whether or not a couple have to pay may depend on the part of the country where they live. Is this a moral issue?

A couple like Jane and Mark will also need to think about the risk of the surrogate mother becoming so attached to the baby she is carrying that she refuses to hand it over. This doesn't happen very often. But if the surrogate mother changes her mind, she can't be forced to give up the child. Legally, she is the mother. This means that if the couple change their mind – perhaps because the baby is born with an unexpected disability – she must look after her child.

To become the child's legal parents the couple have to apply, with the mother's agreement, for a court order, or for adoption. But they need to remember that when their child grows up, he will be able to see his birth certificate, which will still have the surrogate mother's name on it.

> **Sometimes people speculate about women taking part in surrogacy arrangements, although capable of bearing children themselves, because they wish to avoid the physical, social, psychological or financial drawbacks of bearing a child themselves. There is no evidence to suggest that this happens in Britain and it would not be seen as an acceptable use of a surrogacy arrangement.**
>
> *Human Fertilisation & Embryology Authority and British Medical Association*

Should surrogacy be allowed?

Some people believe that the risks of things going wrong with surrogacy arrangements are so great that they should be against the law. But those we know about mostly seem to have turned out well, and it would be almost impossible to prevent private surrogacy arrangements, especially if they just involve 'partial' surrogacy. Sometimes people say that couples for whom surrogacy is the only way left should just accept that they can't have children. Many other childless people have done so and had happy and worthwhile lives. But this is like telling people that suffering is good for them. It only is if they decide for themselves that it is, and if there is no better alternative. If surrogacy is the only way a couple like Jane and Mark can have a child they have to make their own responsible decision about it, just as couples who adopt children have done in the past.

There are ways of acquiring children and a family other than by IVF, AID or surrogacy. One is adoption. This couple have eleven children of various races and backgrounds.

> *A potential surrogate mother must be in good overall health and be able to undergo a pregnancy with the minimum amount of risk to her own health. Some medical conditions will prevent a woman becoming a surrogate mother, for example, if there are any known medical problems which could lead to complications with the pregnancy, or put the woman at risk. Also those who are considerably overweight, are heavy smokers, drinkers, or substance abusers are not suitable as surrogate mothers because of the associated risks both to the woman and the baby.*
>
> *Human Fertilisation and Embryology Authority/British Medical Association*

Birth after death?

But a couple like Jane and Mark are not the only people who may want to have a child by AID, or IVF, or surrogacy. Sperm and fertilised embryos can be frozen and stored. A woman can become pregnant by insemination with the sperm of her dead husband, and a man may want to have an embryo from his wife, after she has died, placed in the womb of a surrogate mother. In Britain this is not allowed unless the husband or wife, before

they died, gave their written consent to it. But even then the doctors involved have to decide for themselves what they think is right. For example, a man might ask the doctors to take eggs from his dead wife, fertilise them with his sperm and place them in a surrogate mother, who will then hand the baby over to the father to bring up. The doctors may feel that it is not in a child's best interests to be born and brought up in this way, and knowing that the man can have other children if he marries again they may refuse to help. They may also be unwilling to help couples whom they think are too old to bring up a child, or couples who want surrogacy because the woman doesn't like the idea of being pregnant for nine months.

Same-sex and single parents?

What if a male or female homosexual couple, or a single woman, want help to have a baby, and the doctors believe that they would be good parents? A male homosexual couple could have a baby by inseminating a surrogate mother with the sperm of one partner. A single woman, or one partner of a female couple, could have a baby by AID. Would it be in the best interests of a child to be born and brought up in this way? Does a child need both a mother and a father? Many widows and widowers have brought their children up very successfully and happily. Would the child of a single woman or a homosexual couple suffer from prejudice or bullying by other children? In the past, many children from racially mixed or divorced families have suffered in this way. But the more such families there are, the less this seems to happen. If more homosexual couples or single women have children will they too be more likely to be accepted? Some are already having children, because AID does not necessarily involve doctors. A male friend may provide a woman with sperm which she can inject into herself. Or a female friend may agree to have the sperm of one of a male couple injected into her so that she can act as a surrogate mother for them.

A lesbian couple awaiting the birth of 'their' child. Should resources be allocated to homosexual couples wanting treatment to enable childbirth?

Government regulation

Doctors are not always involved in these arrangements. But it might be safer if they were. Whether they will be or not, probably will depend on public opinion – on all of us. In Britain, what doctors may do to help people who can't have children is supervised by government regulations and a regulatory body, the Human Fertilisation and Embryology Authority. This means that everything that happens in fertility clinics is carefully controlled. But it can also create problems.

'Spare' embryos

For example, when a couple are going to have a baby by IVF, several eggs may be fertilised. But not all of them will be put back in the woman. The rest will be frozen and stored, in case the first attempt fails and they are needed for a second or third. If these 'spare' embryos are not needed for this, what happens to them? In Britain, the regulations allow some 'spare' embryos to be used in medical research as long as they are not kept alive for more than a couple of weeks, when they will probably die anyway if they are not put in a womb or frozen. But the regulations also say that after some years all the remaining frozen 'spare' embryos must be destroyed.

When this was done a year or so ago many people protested. Some said that it was wrong to destroy fertilised human embryos because that was killing unborn children. For many people, especially in the Roman Catholic Church, the biggest objection to IVF is that it involves creating and then destroying so many human lives. Other people, who believe that a human life does not begin at least until the embryo starts to grow in the womb, think that 'embryo adoption' is the answer. Rather than destroying 'spare' embryos, they should be given to couples who are unable to create embryos for themselves so that they can 'adopt' them as their own.

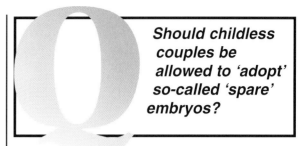

Should childless couples be allowed to 'adopt' so-called 'spare' embryos?

Cloning

Are 'spare' embryos human beings, or are they just a bundle of human cells? This question has become more complicated with the discovery that cells from other parts of the body can be used to clone animals, like Dolly the sheep. In the future, it might be possible to take a cell from Mark, and with an egg from Jane, or a donor, create an embryo which Jane, or a surrogate mother, could carry and give birth to. Such a child would be almost as much like Mark as identical twins are like one another, but, like each of the identical twins, the cloned child would have developed differently and would be a distinct person in his own right.

At present the law does not allow a child to be created by cloning, even if this were scientifically possible in humans. Will it become possible? It might. But scientists would first have to experiment with humans in the ways they have done with sheep – and the risks of the experiments going wrong are too terrible to contemplate. Dolly, for example, was the only lamb born from experiments involving 277 embryos, many of which were abnormal and some of which died after their surrogate mothers gave birth. The scientists who created Dolly have said they would not be willing to do this in humans and cannot imagine that any civilised country would allow it.

How would you feel about being a clone of someone else?

Designer babies

Like cloning, genetic manipulation is a more precise scientific way of 'speeding up' selective breeding, which humans have used for centuries to improve animal and plant stock. Selective breeding, in the form of choosing 'desirable' husbands or wives for their offspring, has also been used by rich and powerful families – often with less successful results. Some people now think that genetic manipulation might be a more reliable way of producing more intelligent or even 'superior' children – sometimes called 'designer babies'. How realistic is this, and is it morally acceptable?

When a gene with a strong link to a serious disease can be identified, it is possible that genetic manipulation or gene therapy might enable scientists to 'knock out' or replace the harmful gene and so prevent the disease. Attempts to do this so far have not been very successful. But they are still in their

If a person is HIV positive should they receive fertility treatment?

In a world of clones, manipulated genes and 'designer babies' there would be many more people who looked identical.

early stages and some inherited diseases are so disabling and distressing that the effort to prevent them in this way is well worth pursuing. It may eventually succeed. But there are still many scientific problems on the way, including the fact that some genes which are harmful in one set of circumstances are beneficial in others.

> **The new technology raises a troubling political question: to whom should we entrust the authority to decide what is a "good" or a "bad" gene? The government? Corporations? University scientists?**
>
> Jeremy Rifkin, president of the Foundation on Economic Trends

> **Proponents of human genetic engineering argue that it would be cruel and irresponsible not to use this powerful new technology to eliminate serious "genetic disorders". However, if diabetes, sickle-cell anaemia and cancer are to be prevented by altering the genetic make-up of individuals, why not proceed to other less serious "disorders": myopia, colourblindness, dyslexia, left-handedness? Why would we ever say no to any alteration of the genetic code that might benefit our offspring?**
>
> Jeremy Rifkin, president of the Foundation on Economic Trends

Attempts to 'improve' people by genetic manipulation are much less realistic and morally acceptable. All human characteristics, including intelligence, are influenced to some extent by our genes. But how intelligent anyone is depends on not just one but many genes, interacting with one another and with the growing organism and its environment in countless complex ways which scientists have not yet even begun to understand. So any attempt to manipulate genes in order to produce people with high intelligence, or 'designer babies' with other desired qualities, again could involve potentially disastrous 'human experiments'.

Such attempts also would presuppose that we know which qualities will be most desirable in the future, for these individuals or for the good of society. But do we? Highly intelligent or handsome people, for example, do not always possess common sense or compassion – qualities which genetic manipulation may never succeed in creating but which, in the end, may be more important for human survival on the planet.

4. TRANSPLANTATION

Alice is a forty-five-year-old musician and composer. Her husband died ten years ago and she has one child, now grown up. Alice also has chronic renal failure. Her kidneys no longer work, and without regular use of dialysis (an artificial kidney machine) she will die. An alternative to dialysis is to have a kidney transplant. Most kidney transplant operations nowadays are very successful. Alice could look forward to a healthier, more normal, and possibly longer, life than on dialysis. Also, in the long run, a successful transplant operation would cost less to the health service.

Cadaver transplants

Most kidneys transplanted in Britain come from a cadaver – a body which has been kept alive artificially for a short time after the brain has died as a result of some catastrophe, such as a road traffic accident, for example. The body should be that of someone who either carried a kidney donor card, or had told other people they wished to be a donor, and whose family do not object. But there are far too few suitable donors for everyone needing a transplant. For every successful kidney transplant operation there are three people like Alice waiting for one.

Transplant Survival Rates (figures in per cent)		
Organ	One Year	Five Years
Kidney	84	70
Liver	62	54
Heart	73	62

Nuffield Council on Bioethics, 1996

A young girl suffering from diabetes undergoing renal dialysis on a kidney machine. Should organs for transplants be more readily available to help solve situations like this?

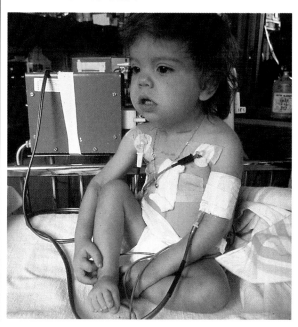

Living donors

There is another possibility. A small proportion of transplanted kidneys come not from dead but from living donors. The most suitable kidney for a successful transplant can be one from a close blood-relative who has two healthy kidneys, and who, if all goes well, can survive comfortably with the remaining one. Alice has never considered asking any member of her own family to help her in this way. But one day her daughter Ann, who is twenty-five and a recently qualified doctor, tells her that she has thought it through very seriously and has decided that she wants Alice to have one of her kidneys. She believes that Alice has a great deal to give the world through her music. If she gets this transplant she will have more time and energy to give to it. Alice's original kidney failure was caused by painkillers which she did not realise were harmful, rather than by any condition Ann is likely to have inherited from her. Ann knows that there are no other members of their family who would be willing or suitable donors.

Ought Alice to agree to Ann's offer? If Ann were ten years younger, Alice's decision might be easier. Someone under sixteen who understands what is involved in an operation and what its likely consequences are, can agree (even if their parents disagree) to it

being done. But the operation needs to be for the young person's own good, especially if it is something as serious as removing a kidney (compared with skin grafts or blood donation, for example). So the surgeons probably wouldn't agree to do it anyway. Occasionally, someone under sixteen has been allowed to donate a kidney to save the life of their much-loved twin brother or sister. Even that is never an easy decision for a parent to agree to. But it is easier than the decision Ann is asking Alice to make.

Costs of kidney treatment

Kidney transplant
Operation: £10,000
Drugs and follow-up treatment
   £3,000 per year

Dialysis
If treatment in hospital £18,000 per year
If treatment at home £11,000 per year

Nuffield Council on Bioethics, 1996

Waiting lists for kidney transplant operations, UK & Republic of Ireland

	Transplants performed	People waiting for transplants
1978	765	1,274
1994	1,744	4,970

Nuffield Council on Bioethics, 1996

In some countries doctors can take kidneys from any suitable brain-dead patient provided they have not actually said in their lifetime that they would object to this. If it makes more organs available and saves more lives, does that justify it?

Opting out and selling kidneys

If Alice lived in another country she might have a better chance of getting a transplant from a non-living donor. In Belgium and Austria, for example, doctors can take kidneys from any suitable brain-dead patient provided they have not actually said in their lifetime that they would object to this. This 'opting out' system seems to make more kidneys available than the British 'opting in' system. If this saves more lives, does that justify it? In other parts of the world, including India (although it is against the law there), poor people may sell one of their kidneys to support their families. In China and Taiwan, kidneys for transplantation are taken from executed criminals. Most national and international medical organisations say that selling kidneys is wrong, and it is against the law in Britain. But if it relieves the poverty of those who sell their kidneys as well as saving the lives of those who receive them, why is it wrong?

In parts of the world, poor people sell one of their kidneys to support their families. Most national and international medical organisations say that selling kidneys is wrong, but if someone decides that doing so improves their life and helps their family, should they be stopped?

Scientists have grown new kidneys in the body cavities of laboratory animals in a breakthrough that promises eventually to enable people to grow replacement organs for their own bodies. The development addresses the two main problems in kidney transplantation: the dire shortage of the organs, and rejection and the use of powerful anti-rejection drugs.

Steve Connor, The Independent, *June 1998*

Organs from animals

In the future, people like Alice and Ann may not have to face these difficult choices. Xenotransplantation from transgenic animals (transplanting kidneys or other organs from animals such as genetically altered pigs) could be an even better alternative than transplants from cadavers or living, related donors. But that will depend both on whether xenotransplantation is shown to be safe and effective, and in many countries on whether religions which regard certain animals as 'unclean' agree to their use in transplantation.

It will also depend on whether society is prepared to breed the large number of transgenic animals that will be required to meet the demand for kidneys, hearts, lungs, livers and other organs. Unlike Dolly the genetically altered sheep, who goes on happily grazing in a field while she produces medicines in her milk, these animals will have to be sacrificed when their organs are needed. Many people already object to the use of animals in existing forms of medical research, and some believe we have no right to inflict new kinds of suffering on them. Perhaps eventually it might become possible, using gene therapy, to repair or regrow damaged organs. But research on this will need to experiment on many animals, and perhaps also human embryos, if it is to be successful. Do the potential benefits justify this?

Q *Is it right to breed animals as a source of organs for transplantation? What is the difference between this and breeding animals for their meat?*

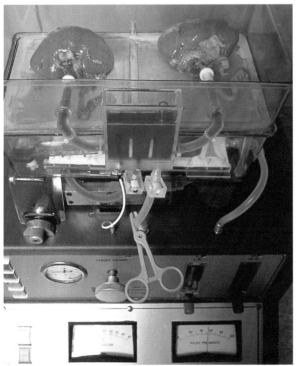

Donor kidneys being preserved in a Max-100 machine during an operation. Would you accept an animal kidney if a human one were unavailable?

5. RATIONING HEALTH CARE

Transplantation is just one of many ways in which medicine today can prolong the life and improve the health of people who in the past would have died young or been chronic invalids. Some ways of saving life are relatively inexpensive – once-fatal infections can be prevented by immunisation, or treated with antibiotics. But many new or better forms of prevention and treatment – drugs or vaccines for HIV and AIDS for example – take a great deal of time and money to develop and cost a great deal to provide.

Waiting for treatment

Family and hospital doctors want to give the best possible treatment to all of their patients. But they also have to work within the budget limits they are given by national government and local health authorities. If they do everything medically possible for each patient as they arrive on the health centre or hospital doorstep, other patients will have to wait, and the queue of waiting patients will get longer and longer. Some of these waiting patients, of course, will just get over whatever is wrong with them – their flu or minor ailments, for example. But others will get worse as their untreated illness progresses and develops complications, so that when they eventually get to see the doctor, treating them will be more time-consuming and expensive than if they had been seen earlier. Others still, whose lives could have been saved or prolonged if they saw the doctor right away, will get so much worse that they die while they are waiting.

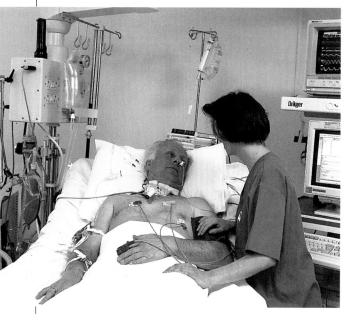

Modern hospitals are full of expensive, high technology equipment. This intensive-care patient is having all his vital signs monitored by machines.

NHS Expenditure by Age, 1993–94	
Age 0–15	£3,722m
Age 16–44	£4,757m
Age 45–64	£3,942m
Age 65-plus	£8,940m

Who comes first?

If everyone has an equal right to health care, queuing for treatment is sometimes inevitable. But it isn't sensible or fair if patients with more serious needs have to wait until those with less serious needs are treated just because they have got ahead of them in the queue. Who to treat first has always been a problem for doctors, especially at a major accident, for example. There, they have to decide which of the victims needs urgent life-saving treatment and help them first, before those who will survive without treatment and also before those who even if they get treatment will probably die anyway. This is never an easy decision for doctors, but they get to know the physical signs which help them to decide in an emergency.

When there is no immediate emergency, however, it is much more difficult. There is usually something that can be done to help almost every patient, and the problem has become increasingly difficult as more and more new and better treatments have been developed. Most people now think that the only way to prevent long and unfair queues building up is to have some kind of rationing – some way of deciding which people in the queue will either not be treated at all, or will at least have to wait longer while others with more important needs are treated first.

The busiest place in any hospital is usually the emergency care area; here a patient with a head injury is being wheeled at speed towards a treatment room.

Q *Have young people a greater right to health care than old people?*

Rationing by age?

But how do you decide who will not be treated, or who will have to wait? In the past, doctors often decided not to give more expensive kinds of hospital treatment to old people because they thought that younger ones were more likely to benefit. But we now know that many old people actually benefit just as much as younger ones from a great variety of treatments, including heart surgery as well as hip replacements. Rationing on the basis of age is not only unfair to old people (ageism) but can be a false economy for the health service. An old person who is not given a hip replacement when they need one, for example, may become so disabled that they need long-term nursing care, which ultimately is more expensive.

It was estimated by a London University study in 1995 that 40,000 people per year have to sell their homes to meet the cost of long-term care.

Michael's angina

Sometimes another kind of rationing is used. Michael is a busy, self-employed plumber in his late fifties. A couple of years ago he began to have chest pains when he was rushing about at work. They usually went away if he sat down or just stood still, but when this began to happen fairly regularly his wife persuaded him to make an appointment with their doctor. After hearing about Michael's symptoms and examining him, the doctor explained

Q *Is it fair that after a lifetime of paying taxes some people might have to use what they have prudently saved for retirement, or even sell their homes, in order to pay for care while those who have not saved get treated for free?*

Life ends at 40 for one in three Africans. Health care has been cut to pay the debt.

Mulima Kufekisa, The Independent,
May 1998

Q *Should smokers be refused surgery? What about people who overeat or overwork or injure themselves rollerblading?*

that his chest pain (angina) was caused by not enough blood getting to his heart muscles because his arteries were furring up (atherosclerosis). The doctor prescribed some tablets which would help to prevent Michael's symptoms and suggested that he should eat less fatty foods and give up smoking.

The tablets worked very well and Michael managed to cut down on cigarettes for a while, but he found it very difficult to give them up completely. Recently Michael's angina returned and last week his doctor told him that the best way to deal with his problem now was to have an angioplasty – an operation to 'rebore' his furred up arteries. But he tells Michael that the local surgeons have decided not to give this operation to anyone who smokes. If Michael can't or won't give up smoking, he will just have to run the risk that his atherosclerosis may eventually lead to a heart attack.

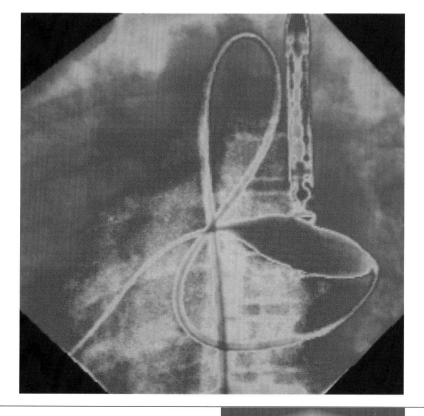

A coloured angiogram of an inflated tube during angioplasty. The vertebrae of the spine and ribs can be seen in the background as the catheter loops around inside the blood vessels of the heart. The tube has expanded at a site where the vessel or heart valve is narrowed and must be widened.

1997	*1-in-6 people are aged 65-plus*
2020	*1-in-5 people will be aged 65-plus*
2030	*1-in-4 people will be aged 65-plus*

The Millennium Papers

A right to treatment?

Are these surgeons right to refuse to treat smokers? Their argument is that the National Health Service (NHS) can only afford a certain number of angioplasty operations and so they have to ration them. The best way to do this is by giving priority to patients who are most likely to benefit, and patients who continue to smoke are in general less likely to benefit. It is like rubbing salt into a wound. Michael agrees that smoking is bad for his health, but he feels that it helps him relax and he really does find it almost impossible to give up. He reckons, too, that all the income tax and tobacco tax he has paid over the years entitles him to an operation which is likely to prolong his life, even if not for as long as it might if he gave up smoking. Hasn't he earned the right to it?

Michael's doctor also wonders if the surgeons are right. Non-smokers as well as smokers get atherosclerosis, and smoking is only one of the factors, however important, that determine how well patients do after angioplasty. Michael's place in the queue might be taken by a non-smoker who for some other reason will benefit less from it than he would have done. The doctor hopes that Michael will be able to give up smoking so that he can get the operation. But if he doesn't, and the operation is refused, there is no guarantee that this will

Many people believe that those who wilfully neglect their health through smoking should go to the back of the queue for health care resources. Smokers argue that the taxes they pay on their tobacco entitle them to non-discriminatory treatment.

save money for the NHS. If and when Michael eventually has a heart attack, or several heart attacks, there will then be no question of refusing him the emergency treatments and longer term care he needs. In the long run this may turn out to be more expensive than giving him an angioplasty.

> *Why shouldn't people have to pay directly for their own health care?*

A bottomless pit?

How to ration health care is one of the biggest moral dilemmas facing society today. People often say that more money should be put into the health service to give more patients the treatment they need. Nobody denies that more money would help. But some people say that health care is a bottomless pit – if more money and treatments are provided, expectations rise and even more is

then needed. Politicians reckon that we are not willing to pay the taxes needed to provide this. Are they right? How important is health care compared with all the other things – education, transport, defence, law and order – that also are paid for by taxation?

> *Last year 4,000 people died due to heroin use in this country [USA]; 400,000 people died due to tobacco use. The vast majority of those people started using tobacco when they were kids.*
>
> Arthur Caplan, US Bioethicist, Due Consideration, *Chichester, Wiley 1998*

> *How important is health care compared with all the other things – education, transport, defence, law and order – that also are paid for by taxation?*

6. DYING WELL

Mr Smith is eighty-nine and has lived in a nursing home since his second stroke. A stroke 'strikes' someone when part of their brain is damaged by being deprived of blood as a result either of internal bleeding or of a blocked blood vessel. Strokes can vary in seriousness, depending on what parts of the brain are damaged and how badly. At worst, a stroke can be fatal, or can leave someone paralysed down one side and unable to see, speak or understand properly. But strokes are often much less serious than this, and people, even of Mr Smith's age and older, can recover from them. Mr Smith himself recovered almost completely from his first stroke three years ago. But his second, a year later, was more serious, and although his speech is almost back to normal he is now too physically disabled to look after himself properly.

Mr Smith did not like the idea of selling his house and moving into a nursing home after his stroke, but he accepted it as inevitable. His wife died several years ago, his daughter lives with her husband and children in Australia, and his son is an unmarried war correspondent who spends a lot of time with him whenever he is back in Britain. After the stroke his son considered getting a home-based job, but his father talked him out of it. The nursing home was comfortable, he could still

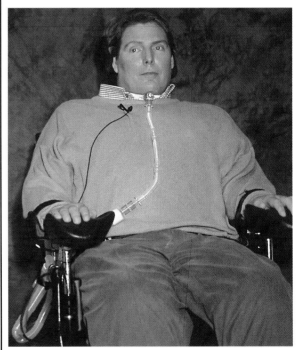

Christopher Reeve, the actor who played Superman, was leading a fit and active outdoor life one day, the next day he was a paraplegic following a riding accident. Presented with such an abrupt transformation, should we be entitled to decide we no longer wish to continue with our life?

read and listen to music on his radio, and a number of his former colleagues visited him regularly. Many of them still think of him as Professor Schmidt, the famous physicist. But when he came to Britain as a refugee in the 1930s, he changed his name to Smith, and when he arrived in the nursing home he decided that it would be easier all round if he was just called 'Mr' Smith.

> **. . .it would not be possible to frame adequate safeguards against non-voluntary euthanasia if voluntary euthanasia were to be legalised . . . We are also concerned that vulnerable people – the elderly, lonely, sick or distressed – would feel pressure, whether real or imagined, to request early death.**
>
> *House of Lords Select Committee on Medical Ethics, January 1994*

Allowing someone to die in peace

Because the nursing home is quite near his old house, Mr Smith is still looked after by his own doctor, who is also a good friend. After he settles in at the nursing home, they have a long talk. Mr Smith knows that at some point he may have another stroke, or perhaps a heart attack, and that his slow-growing cancer may eventually spread. His doctor knows that Mr Smith is Jewish and that most Jewish religious teachers believe that everything medically possible should be done to prolong life, at least until it is clear that someone is actually dying. But as Mr Smith reminds the doctor, he has never been very orthodox in his Jewish beliefs. In fact he agrees with those Buddhists who say that dying is as natural as living and should be as peaceful as possible. So if and when he does develop some life-threatening condition he hopes that his doctor will not fight it, but do whatever is possible to make him comfortable and allow him to die in peace.

To treat or not to treat

The doctor is sad that his old friend no longer wants to go on living. But he recognises that Mr Smith is not depressed but at peace with himself, and that he knows what he wants. So he promises to do as he says. Then a few months later, as winter approaches, the matron of the nursing home asks the doctor if he will give Mr Smith an injection of flu vaccine. The other residents' doctors are doing this, and the risk of infection spreading is greater if everyone is not immunised. The doctor knows that many specialists in the care of the elderly don't agree with the matron's view on this. He also knows that if Mr Smith gets flu it may well go on to pneumonia, and he may then die without too much discomfort if he is given good medical and nursing care.

Should the doctor try to persuade Mr Smith to have the flu vaccine for the sake of the other patients? Or should he tell the matron that, knowing what he does about Mr Smith's views, he is not prepared even to ask him? Even if he does ask him, of course, it will still be up to Mr Smith to decide. It would be illegal to give him the flu vaccine or any other treatment against his expressed wishes, just as it would be illegal for a doctor to give a blood transfusion to an adult Jehovah's Witness who says that he does not want it because it is against his religious beliefs.

A thoughtful old lady in a nursing home. Such places can be lonely and depressing and many elderly people decline rapidly compared to when they live on their own. How would we ensure that euthanasia did not become a means of saving money on care for the elderly?

> **Caring for an old person in a nursing home costs nearly £18,000 a year. The government pays only if they have less than £16,000 left. Every year 40,000 elderly people who go into nursing homes have to sell their homes to pay the costs. Most of them believed that the NHS would look after everyone "from cradle to grave."**
>
> *Private health care advertisement*

Best interests and living wills

The doctor's decision might have been more difficult if Mr Smith had been deprived of speech and understanding by another stroke. Then it would be up to the doctor to decide what is in his best interests. But even then the doctor would have a duty to take into account what Mr Smith had told him in the past. When doctors have to decide whether they are going to resuscitate patients who are no longer able to express their own wishes, they are expected to find out as much as they can from the patient's friends and relatives about any wishes the patient may have expressed on the subject. Some patients write a 'living will' or 'advance directive' saying what they would want to be done, and if these statements clearly state that the patient does not want to be treated in a particular way, it can be illegal for doctors to go against them.

Permanent vegetative state

Sometimes there is no way of knowing what the patient would have wanted. Patients in a permanent vegetative state (a form of unconsciousness caused by severe brain injury), for example, are often quite young. Unlike older people such as Mr Smith, they may never have considered the possibility in advance. Doctors and the courts found it very difficult to decide what was in the best interests of Tony Bland, who was left unconscious after being crushed at the Hillsborough football ground disaster.

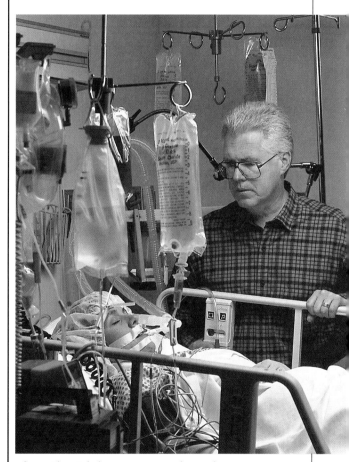

A patient lying unconscious in neurological intensive care. It is difficult to predict the outcome for people in comas and an agonising decision for relatives if offered the choice of not continuing artificial feeding.

Part of the difficulty is that it can be hard for doctors to be certain, at least for the first few months, how much consciousness may be left. Patients with a condition which may look similar, the locked-in syndrome, are highly conscious of everything going on around them but are unable to communicate, except perhaps by blinking an eyelid. That was how the French journalist Jean-Dominique Bauby, for example, communicated with the interpreter who wrote down his amazing book *The Diving-Bell & the Butterfly*.

Even when doctors are sure that the patient is in a true permanent vegetative state from which they will never recover, the decision about how to treat them can still be very difficult. When someone like Mr Smith suffers serious brain damage after a further severe stroke, it may only be a matter of time until they get a life-threatening infection. If that happens, doctors do not necessarily have to try to cure the infection with antibiotics for example, but can make the patient as comfortable as possible until they die.

But patients in a permanent vegetative state may survive such infections. The question then is whether it is better to go on, or to stop providing the artificial feeding through a tube or drip that is keeping their bodies alive. The courts have decided that it is not against the law for doctors to discontinue artificial feeding. But other people say that food and water are not a form of medical treatment, like antibiotics, but basic necessities of life which should always be given.

> *Paralysed from head to toe, the prisoner is imprisoned inside his own body, his mind intact, but unable to speak or move. In my case, blinking my left eyelid is my only means of communication. . . something like a giant invisible diving-bell holds my whole body prisoner. . . my mind takes flight like a butterfly. . .*
>
> *J-D Bauby*, The Diving-Bell and the Butterfly, *Fourth Estate, London, 1997*

The principle of double effect

Some people say that withdrawing either antibiotics or feeding, or even giving painkillers which may shorten life, is 'passive euthanasia'. But most people, including most doctors, and also the law, regard these ways of allowing a patient to die, or assisting a patient to die well, as very different from actively assisting a patient to die, or euthanasia. Even the Roman Catholic Church, which is very 'pro-life', teaches that doctors need not prolong life by 'extraordinary' or 'disproportionate' means of treatment which will only prolong a patient's suffering. Many doctors and others, not necessarily religious believers, also subscribe to the Catholic principle of double effect, which says that doctors may relieve pain or suffering with painkillers, even if this shortens the patient's life, so long as the doctor's overriding and sincere intention is to relieve pain and not deliberately to end life. This is very different from what most people mean by euthanasia.

Being old does not mean you cannot continue to enjoy life or contribute something to others. Project Chronos has investigated human ageing and discovered genes which influence it. One day it might be possible to prolong the average healthy lifespan to more than 100 years. But in an already crowded world with limited resources, would that be desirable?

> **The church and the law should be separate. If you disagree with voluntary euthanasia don't use it, but please don't deny the right to me to use it if I want to.**
>
> *Man who became the first person to commit assisted suicide under the voluntary euthanasia law in Darwin, Australia*

Asking for euthanasia

Miss Brown is a ninety-year-old retired journalist, who lives alone. She is highly intelligent, but is almost blind and has become increasingly forgetful over the past few years. Recently she fell asleep in front of a gas fire and burnt her legs quite badly. She is now in hospital for treatment of the burns and they are beginning to improve. When one of the junior doctors she particularly likes comes to see her, she tells her that she is grateful for the treatment but she doesn't want to go on. She isn't depressed, just tired of the effort of going on living and ready to die.

Above all she doesn't want to become really demented. She has always believed that euthanasia would be the right thing in these circumstances, and she knows that doctors can sometimes do it quietly. Can the doctor help her?

The doctor is taken aback. She knows that Miss Brown is not depressed, but she also knows that what she is asking for is against the law. Euthanasia literally means 'a good death' or 'dying well'. But what the word usually refers to nowadays is a doctor deliberately killing someone in order to end their pain or suffering. Just about the only place in the world where this is officially allowed is in the Netherlands. Doctors there may give a lethal injection to a patient, but only as a last resort if the patient is experiencing intolerable suffering with no prospect of improvement, and if the patient persistently requests it. Occasionally in Britain, when someone is dying in great pain, and for some reason is not getting proper medical and nursing care, a member of their family, in desperation, has smothered or poisoned them. But this 'mercy-killing', as it is called, still counts as murder, even if the courts sometimes impose only a light sentence.

> **Let me die like the poor people I help.**
>
> *Mother Teresa, Calcutta*

> *The right to die is an integral part of our right to control our own destinies so long as the rights of others are not affected. That right should, in my opinion, include the ability to enlist assistance from others, including the medical profession, in making death as painless and quick as possible.*
>
> Judge Compton in US
> case of Bouvia v Superior Court

Euthanasia, doctors and the law

What Miss Brown is asking for is something the doctor cannot really agree to. Her pain from the burns is under control and there is no medical reason to give her the amount of pain-killers that would be needed to end her life. Quite possibly she is suffering from the early stages of dementia, but she is otherwise physically fit for her age and could live well into her nineties. Even if the doctor was willing to do it, she could not give her a lethal injection in hospital without having to account for it. The doctor would then have to be tried for murder or attempted murder, which would probably end her medical career and her ability to help other people who are suffering.

The doctor tries to explain all this to Miss Brown as sensitively as possible, and she says she understands. A week later she is well enough to go home. Six months later the doctor discovers her in another ward in the hospital with serious liver damage as a result of a paracetamol overdose. She had tried to kill herself and might have succeeded, but an old friend turned up unexpectedly to visit her and called the police and an ambulance when she suspected something might be wrong.

Should euthanasia be allowed?

Miss Brown will die eventually, either as a result of her liver damage or from an infection which doctors may decide not to fight. But the junior doctor wonders why this tired old lady had to go through so much mental as well as physical suffering on the way. Might it not be better if euthanasia were made legal, or at least if doctors were allowed to give someone like Miss Brown the right amount of the best drugs to use in order to end her own life successfully? But although suicide and attempted suicide are no longer against the law, a doctor assisting suicide in this way might still be prosecuted. Actively helping a patient like Miss Brown to die also goes against what many doctors feel to be their professional duty: 'to cure sometimes, to relieve often, to comfort always', but not to kill.

Q *Is it acceptable not to treat a curable illness in the knowledge that the patient may die as a result, even if it is what the patient wishes?*

Q *When doctors' knowledge of severe brain damage is relatively limited, is it right that decisions are taken about which patients should live and which should die?*

A disabled competitor participating in a marathon. Many thousands of people continue to make the most of their lives despite the most incredible physical handicaps.

The 'slippery slope'

Why is euthanasia against the law and medical ethics in Britain and most other countries? The main reason usually given by people who believe it should be against the law is the 'slippery slope' argument. This supposes that if euthanasia is allowed in the exceptional cases when pain and suffering cannot be relieved, it will soon be allowed in cases where they can be relieved by other means but doctors and families

are not trying hard enough. If it is accepted that people like Miss Brown have a right to be helped to die, other vulnerable old people who want to go on living will then begin to feel they have a duty to ask to be helped to die, so that they are not a burden to their families for example. If doctors are allowed to kill patients who request it, they will soon be killing people who do not request it but are a burden on the health service – just as happened under the Nazis.

Is the 'slippery slope' argument right? People who support euthanasia say that these harmful consequences of legalising it are very unlikely in a democratic country nowadays, especially if there are proper regulations about when it is to be allowed. If these regulations say that the person requesting euthanasia has to be experiencing intolerable suffering with no prospect of improvement, that might still mean that a doctor would have to refuse euthanasia to someone like Miss Brown, although

they might be allowed to give her a more effective means of ending her own life than that she chose.

Two sides of the argument

Whether or not euthanasia is ever legalised in Britain will depend on public opinion. At present politicians tend to avoid the subject because public opinion is too deeply divided. The arguments and those supporting them on both sides are very powerful, perhaps equally powerful. Most religions are officially opposed to euthanasia, saying for example that God alone should decide when our lives are to end. But many religious as well as non-religious people believe that when there is really no other way to prevent great suffering, euthanasia is not necessarily wrong or against the will of God. Would legalising euthanasia lead down the 'slippery slope'? Or are doctors and the rest of us good and wise enough to use permission for euthanasia and assisted suicide only when it is necessary and right to do so?

GLOSSARY

abortion deliberately ending a pregnancy and the life of a foetus. When this happens naturally it is called a miscarriage

AID artificial insemination by donor, fertilising a woman's eggs with sperm provided by a man other than her partner

angina chest pain caused by not enough blood getting to the heart muscles

angioplasty an operation to widen an artery narrowed by disease

atherosclerosis furring up of the arteries through which blood flows from the heart

cadaver a dead body, or one kept alive artificially for a short time after brain death

clone an individual with the same genes as another individual

dialysis an artificial substitute for the function of the kidneys

Down's syndrome a genetic condition causing some degree of mental disability

embryo describes the stage of human growth up to twelve weeks after fertilisation

euthanasia giving someone in pain a deadly drug to help them to die, literally means 'dying well'

foetus describes the stage of human growth from twelve weeks after fertilisation until birth

gamete term used for both sperm and eggs

gene a unit of inheritance, passed on from parent to offspring

IVF *in vitro* fertilisation, fertilising eggs outside a woman's body in a laboratory

kidneys a pair of organs which regulate blood and water in the body (people can survive without one kidney, but not without both)

living will a statement about how someone wants to be treated if they were to become gravely ill

locked-in syndrome a medical condition when someone is paralysed but conscious

permanent vegetative state a medical condition when someone is unconscious but appears to sleep, wake and react to noises, etc.

resuscitation treatment to save life after a heart attack or other life-threatening event

stroke damage to the brain when deprived of normal blood flow

surrogate a woman who carries a foetus in her womb for another couple

transplantation planting bodily tissues or organs taken from one body into another body

xenotransplantation transplantation from an animal ('xeno' means a stranger)

INDEX